Local Marketing for Small Business

Building a 5 Star Reputation

The Essential Guide to Attracting
a Flood of New Business

Clarence Williams, PMP

Get a FREE Competitive Analysis by going to

http://LocalMarketingForSmallBusiness.com

Published by: Push Button Publishing

http://pushbutton-publishing.com/

Push Button Local Marketing, LLC

11877 Douglas Rd. Ste 102

Johns Creek, GA 30005

Copyright © 2013 Clarence Williams, PMP

ISBN-10: 0989279057
ISBN-13: 978-0-9892790-5-5

DEDICATION

This book was written for small business owners who approach their industry as business people and contributors to the local economy and business community. If you expect to be a competitive and successful small business owner in your chosen industry, then local marketing has become essential to your online efforts.

The most competitive small business owners are finding an increasing number of ways to improve their online marketing results. With products that allow for target specific campaigning, implementing effective marketing strategies and using the right tools can help you carefully track results while maximizing your ROI with every campaign launched. You can get everything you need to know here.

This is also a must read if you are hiring someone else to do your marketing. The things in this book are things you should know before you hire someone else to do it for you. Knowing this information will save you a tremendous amount of money in the future.

CONTENT

TERMS AND CONDITIONS
LEGAL NOTICE

BUILDING A 5 STAR REPUTATION

Do You Know What People Are Saying About Your Business Online?

The most important thing that you can protect is your professional reputation as a small business owner. This should be your starting place for local marketing. Proactively marketing, monitoring and managing your business' online reputation is critical to your local success. The process involves being aware of what is being said about you, guarding and enhancing your online reputation, and in some cases, repairing malicious and derogatory comments made by unhappy customers or unscrupulous competitors. Here is a basic guide to safeguarding your business' good name online.

The Internet has changed the way we view reputations. Today, you can conduct an online search on any of your friends and immediately find out what they did last weekend and whom they did it with. You can find photos, videos and much more from the comfort and secrecy of your own home. Not only can you do this with friends, but you can do it with businesses too.

Want to find a great Chinese food place? Do a quick search on Yelp.com or Yellowpages.com and within seconds you will have pages of results. These results will all have reviews posted by current or former customers, and within seconds you can form an opinion about a business that you may have never even heard of, except for what you are learning about at that moment online.

While this advance in technology has allowed us to connect on a level never before possible, it has also brought with it a laundry list of negatives. The problem isn't necessarily the technology itself, but rather the speed with which the information it yields enters our lives.

The Internet has turned into the American Wild West of old. The expansion of the Internet is outrunning and outgunning law enforcement, social norms and even everyday ethics. Anybody with an Internet connection and a keyboard can say anything they want to, about whomever they want to all while typically avoiding any type of accountability, repercussions, or in some cases, deserved criminal punishment.

Imagine a world where it was possible for a major corporation to send a single email to YouTube forcing them to remove 50,000 videos due to copyright infringement. However, if someone were to post a scandalous video of you or your family, you would likely have no legal power to remove it. Seems like an unfair and lopsided world, doesn't it? Welcome to the current Internet age that we live in.

Hackers, angry customers, competitors, ex-spouses and other malicious types are all able to take advantage of the loopholes in legal protection and have their say, no matter how bad it might be. Meanwhile, businesses and everyday people alike are being take advantage of from fraudulent, slanderous and sometimes violent communications on the web.

Unfortunately, the law has lagged behind the expansion of the Internet. Just like those pioneer towns of the American Wild West, we as Internet users must find a way, to keep our businesses, reputation and livelihoods safe from others.

This is where Reputation Marketing & Management comes in.

What Is Reputation Marketing & Management?

Online Reputation Marketing & Management is so much more than what the title suggests. Reputation managers will monitor any communications that might be happening about a particular brand. If they notice something negative that requires attention, they will apply their broad and vast knowledge of Internet marketing techniques to ensure that the problem is fixed.

You could think of reputation managers as part customer service rep and part online marketer. The goal of Reputation Marketing & Management is not to squelch the honest feedback of customers, but to ensure that damages resulting from negative falsities are minimized and that the company is being accurately represented online.

These negative online implications can come easier than you might think. For instance, anybody can start a blog. There are literally hundreds of free blogging platforms that people can use. If an ex-employee or a competitor wanted to start a blog that was meant to spread lies about your business or even about you personally, they could do it. In fact, this practice happens all too often, thanks to the Internet making it so easy to do so. It is the job of the reputation manager to ensure that problems like this are dealt with quickly, properly and professionally.

10 ONLINE REPUTATION MARKETING & MANAGEMENT FACTS YOU NEED TO KNOW

1. **Fortune 500 Company Executives Believe In Reputation Marketing & Management.**

   "58% of executives believe that Reputation Marketing & Management should be addressed, but only 15% actually do anything about it" – Deloitte. You want to get a competitive edge? Start DOING what nearly 60% of big time executives say they SHOULD be doing but aren't!

2. **Professional Marketers Say "Trust" Is Number One for Making a Sales-Worthy Impression.**

   "84% of marketers believe that building trust will be the primary focus for marketing efforts in the future" – Deloitte. Most marketers feel that trust is what makes the sale. Do you trust someone with a bad reputation? Neither will your customers.

3. **MOST People Use Social Media to Decide What to Buy.**

   "4 out of 5 people state that they have received advice via social media regarding what product or service to purchase." It is no secret. Social proof is powerful. If your social media reputation is lacking, you lose.

4. More and More Large Companies Are Hiring Full-Time Online Reputation Managers.

"The US Bureau of Labor Statistics puts the average salary of an online reputation manager between $38,000–$72,000." – Labor Dept. Want to know what big companies think about Reputation Marketing & Management? According to the Bureau of Labor Statistics they think highly enough of reputation managers to hire them full-time and pay them handsome salaries.

5. More Adults Are On Social Media Sites Than You Might Think.

"46% of online adults have created their own profile on a social networking site." We can't dismiss social media as a young person's world anymore. All the people with the money and the spending power are moving online and making decisions based on what they find there.

6. The Public Trusts Social Media.

"Half of online adults (48%) agree that getting to know new people now is easier and more meaningful because you can learn things online about the people you meet." Do you ever wish your customers could get to know you better? If they knew you better, they might buy more of your products and/or services. They can, and they want to via social media!

7. More Than You Know...

"16% of all Internet users have looked online for more information about someone they were dating or in a relationship with." Think about that for a second! Even the most personal parts of our lives are affected by our online reputation.

8. **People Are Using Social Media To Gain An Edge On Their Competition. That Means You.**

   "31% of employed Internet users have searched online for information about co-workers, professional colleagues or business competitors."

9. **Employees Feel Pressure to Manage Their Online Reputation.**

   "12% of employed adults say they need to market themselves online as part of their job." If 1 out of every 10 employees thinks they need to be building their online reputation, shouldn't you as a business owner be acting in the same capacity?

10. **Social Proof Reigns Supreme and Traditional Advertising Is Dying.**

    "78% of consumers trust peer recommendations, only 14% trust advertisements." Guess what, your reputation goes before you and social media only ensures that. No matter what ads you are running, no matter how many banners you put on your storefront, it will be the recommendations of peers based on your reputation that will bring customers, who are ready to buy, right to your doorstep.

The Final Frontier

While the Internet reputation battlefield rages on, business owners only have one of two clear choices:

> **Choice A:** Refuse to take your business online and miss out on the huge potential that so many other businesses are experiencing.

> **Choice B:** Proceed with caution into the final frontier using Internet marketing and reap the rewards for making such a smart move.

Protecting your reputation online is a must if you plan to survive as a Small business in this competitive environment. With the help of a professional online reputation manager, you can turn the Internet Wild West into the virtual gold rush. Manage your online reputation and you will make money from your online efforts.

To Check Out Your Reputation for FREE
Go To
http://www.MyReputationDenders.com

LOCAL MARKETING SECRETS EXPOSED

Learn The Secrets That Most Marketing Consultants Would Not Want You To Know.

Let's face it, every small business owner in your industry can't be listed at the top of the local search results when someone is searching for chiropractic services in your area. Showing up first in the results is challenge and only one listing can be number one in each area. Even being on the first page of the results is challenging if you are in a competitive market area. It is important to note that you can do everything right and still not show up on the front page of the search results. The reason for this is simple, the search engines own their algorithms for local search and no one (except for the search engines themselves) knows the right formula for being number one in the results. But there's good news! **You can absolutely dominate the local results if you study your competition.** *That's the secret, if you study very specific elements of the other Small business owner in your industry that are on the first page in your area, you will have all you need to realistically compete with them.*

This is probably one of the most critical points in this book. Having access to the right tools that will allow you to analyze your fellow small business owners will practically give you an seemingly unfair advantage in your area. Typically, the search engines reward small businesses with optimized, content rich websites that have relevant, keyword based information about the services being provided. But that's only a small part of the local marketing game. There are other (more important) things that need to be in place if you intend to compete and win.

Below are basic tips you should know if you expect to be rewarded with first page rankings in any local area:

Tips on choosing your first social media site to use

<u>Go find and claim the websites that the local search engines have already created for you.</u> The three major search engines (Google, Bing and Yahoo) have probably already created a website for you. These sites are essential because each of the search engines will reward their own listing of your chiropractic firm if you have properly claimed optimized the listing they have created for you . This is a critical point. In other words, the local site that they have created for you is more important than the website you have created. If you are the do it yourself kind of person, you can go directly to each of these search engines and signup.

- **Google** - http://www.google.com/business/placesforbusiness/

- **Yahoo** - http://smallbusiness.yahoo.com/local-listings/

- **Bing** - https://www.bingplaces.com/

WARNING!!!

<u>There is something you should know before you sign up.</u> Simply signing up to these sites will not necessarily get you on the first page of the search engines. There are simply things you will need before you start the signup process.

- *Your Name, Address and Phone number (NAP).* It is important you provide a correct and consistent NAP information to each of the search engines.

- *The categories that your business falls within.* For a typical small business, that's usually something similar to "Industry > Speciality>Product or Service".

- *A short and concise description of your chiropractic firm.* About 150 words should work.

- *Your business hours.* Make sure that your business hours consistently across all three search engines.

- *Payment Methods.* You will have to indicate if you accept cash, check, major credit cards or any other form of financing.

- *Email address and website information.* Although it's not absolutely necessary that you already have a website, having at least a simple one page site about your business will add to the likelihood that your firm will have a higher ranking in the search engines listings.

- *Logos, Videos and Pictures.* These three things are usually not "required" by the search engines to claim your pages. But they are an essential part of the local optimization process. A few other things that make a big difference in local ranking results is if the following items are also provided:

  o A listing of your products and services

  o Any social event calendars

  o Staff bios

<u>Use a service to get this done.</u> Keep in mind that although you can setup all of the above things yourself, I don't recommend it. You will save lots of time and effort if you use the right automated tools or hire someone who knows what they are doing to do it for you. There are three companies that I recommend using to get this done. Each of them have their own unique advantages. Since they have overlapping services, you really don't need to use all three. The biggest value that these companies bring to the table is that they will setup additional local search engines and directories that are not as prominent but are critical to list with as well if you expect to be successful in the local marketing game.

- **Yext** - Provides local cloud-computing services for marketers to manage their geodata and local content and connect it everywhere. When marketers enter local data or content like a phone number, photo, or offer in the Yext Cloud, it updates on connected search engines, ad networks, listings sites and more. This enables marketing organizations to seamlessly deliver relevant geodata, pictures, posts, prices, inventory, offers, updates and more on any service connected to their local cloud. For more information on Yext services go to **http://PBLM.NET/yext**

- **Universal Business Listing** - a service of UBL Interactive, is an established leader in the booming online marketing sector of location-based search, with over 100,000 businesses using our services. UBL helps business owners get their business listed correctly in major search engines, online yellow pages, social networks, directory sites, 411 and 118 information services, vertical search engines, industry directories, mobile apps, and GPS navigation services. For more information on Universal Business Listing services go to **http://pblm.co/14**

- **neustar/Localeze** - This company will get your practice noticed in local search listings. That's because Neustar® Localeze® has direct, authorized relationships with over 100 local search platforms. They have a continuous optimization process includes rigorous data cleansing, verification, normalization, organization and synonym mapping. For more information neustar/Localeze services go to **http://pblm.co/15**.

The real name of the game is having the right citations. Citations are defined as "mentions" of your business name, address and phone number on other webpages, even if there is no link to your internet site. An example of a citation might be an online yellow pages directory where your company is detailed, however not linked to. It can likewise be a regional chamber of commerce, or a neighborhood business association where your company details can be discovered, even if they are not connecting at all to your website. You could also see the term "web references" utilized on various other websites which is synonym for "citations".

Citations are an essential element of the ranking algorithms of the significant online search engine. Various other factors being equal, companies with a greater number of citations will probably place higher than companies with fewer citations.

Citations from reputable and well-indexed websites (like Superpages.com for instance) assistance enhance the degree of certainty the online search engine have about your business's contact information and categorization. To paraphrase previous Arizona Cardinals' coach Dennis Environment-friendly, citations help search engines verify that companies" are who we thought they were!".

Citations are particularly crucial in the chiropractic industry where numerous providers don't have sites themselves. Without much other details, the search engines count heavily on whatever information they can find on the web about businesses.

Citations likewise validate that a business belongs to a community. It's tough for someone to fake membership in a chamber of commerce or a city or county business index, or to be discussed in a regional online paper or popular blog site. Citations (and links) from these sort of websites can considerably enhance your Regional search engine rankings.

<u>Doing the following will set you apart from your peers.</u> There are some little known service providers who will research your competition locally to determine who your top competing small businesses are and make sure you are listed with the same websites. This is really the dirty little secret to dominating a local area.

So - if you were a small business owner in Atlanta, Georgia, there are a top 40+ local citation sources.

Some of the most important citation sources for businesses in Atlanta

www.switchboard.com	www.foursquare.com
www.golocal247.com	www.yellowpagecity.com
www.411.com	www.yext.com
www.teez.it	www.mapquest.com
www.merchantcircle.com	www.phonenumber.com
www.yellowise.com	www.showmelocal.com
www.local.com	www.yelp.com
www.localdatabase.com	www.yellowbot.com
local.yahoo.com	www.uscity.net
www.yext.com	www.pennysaverusa.com
www.superpages.com	wheretoapp.com
www.yext.com	www.tupalo.co
www.factual.com	www.citysquares.com
www.citysearch.com	www.yext.com

www.yasabe.com

www.yext.com

www.yext.com

www.yext.com

www.pocketly.com

www.mojopages.com

www.getfave.com

www.elocal.com

www.americantowns.com

www.foursquare.com

www.chamberofcommerce.com

www.topix.com

www.8coupons.com

www.whitepages.com

www.bing.com

www.localpages.com

www.yellowmoxie.com

www.coreapi.citymaps.com

www.facebook.com

www.plus.google.com

So if you practice in Atlanta, Georgia and you signed up for the above listed websites, have already properly optimized your own website and the sites provided by the three major search engines, you can reasonably expect to have a fighting chance at competing locally with the small businesses currently at the top of the search rankings.

Warning: keep in mind that although this is a critical step, it's still only a piece of the local marketing puzzle. Read on because the rest of this book covers some of the other major strategies you will need to implement in order to compete with the "Big Boys" in your area. If your practice is outside of Atlanta, these are not necessarily the sites that will help you dominate the search engines. You can get a customized list of sites by going to the Here (http://pblm.co/16) and submitting a request. You will be provided with a list of your competitors and the local sites that they are currently listed on to achieve first page and number one rankings in your area.

The following pages in this book will focus on video, social, mobile and basic SEO strategies that you should consider when putting together a strategy to dominate your local market. These are really some of the more popular forms of local marketing and will probably give you the best return on investment. However, this book was not intended to cover all of the online strategies available. It was developed as a reference guide of some of the more popular strategies used by local marketing professionals or consultants. These are things you can implement yourself and reserve some of your marketing dollars for your paid advertising campaigns.

Disclaimer: Push Button Local Marketing, LLC (the sponsor of this book) is a affiliated with the above listed partners. These are the exact services it uses to service its own clients. The company does receive a financial benefit if you go to the links and use the above listed services.

HARNESS THE POWER OF VIDEO

How To Use Video Marketing To Grow Your Business Online

With the growth of the Internet and technology, videos have increasingly become a more powerful tool in acquiring more leads and growing one's business. The commercialization of video editing tools and ease of sharing videos through video sharing sites like YouTube have made the growth of the video industry suddenly explode. Presently, it doesn't matter if you are a small time marketer or a corporate giant; you stand to gain a great deal through leveraging videos to grow your business. You can find all the info you need here.

Marketing a product or service well is the basis of any promotional campaign. As there are many ways of doing this, and getting the product to a platform where it's generally recognizable, serious thought must also be given to the mode of adverting utilized. Video might be able to assist you with that.

Getting Started With Video

The effect of video presentations as an online promotion strategy is being felt in a big way by marketers. Individuals who are promoting their networks online are utilizing these videos to drive their point straight home and make a genuine impression on the visitors. Better overall conversion rates are typically the result in the end.

The Basics

Videos are simple to make and even easier to upload. They can convey a lot more than simple typed words can. This is the primary reason so many marketers are going all out to market their products and/or services using web video marketing.

The technique is fairly straightforward - make an appealing video about your product or service. Give the viewer some sort of info, and put it on a relevant place online where it might end up on a website, blog or even a social media community network. The video is advertized in several ways so that it gets a large number of viewers, who all see the brand name of the product or the link of a website, or even both. This type of visual messaging means that individuals who watch the video are more likely to purchase the product than the individuals who merely read the text on a site.

For local business, the concept of video marketing works wonderfully. The following are a few reasons why it does exceptionally well here:

1. It builds up the credibility of a business because, in most cases, individuals will be able to see and hear the business in the video. This adds authenticity to the business' services and/or products.

2. It helps explain the concept in a different and improved way. Many people prefer to see, hear and comprehend over reading and trying to understand. Because video contains various visual effects, such as illustrations, it might be easier and more pleasant for a viewer to see and understand versus standard text.

3. Facial gestures and motions mean a lot to individuals who are considering spending cash, time and effort on a business. They may see these types of gestures in a video. Therefore, the business becomes more real to them, and they will perhaps feel less anxious about it.

4. Videos may also help in branding. Hearing you speak the name of your business makes it sound more believable, so there's a greater chance that the name will have a recall value. This is a way of branding your products and/or services, which is far better than merely writing your business name down on your website.

In every way that you look at it, video works exceptionally well for marketing. People in business must take the time to understand this concept and utilize it for their promotional needs. Video marketing has been demonstrated time and time again to be among the most useful tools in being able to successfully accomplish the presence the product and/or service needs in order to be remarkably recognizable.

Video marketing brings life to any marketing campaign as it has the power to transform static and unattractive conventional ad styles into action orientated presentations. In the fast moving and ever evolving world of today, individuals are looking for fresh and new ways to capture the attention of the market share of buyers and, likewise, customers want to be wooed with exciting displays that delight their minds and senses.

Video marketing has the unique element of being able to connect with a target audience both visually and mentally, taking the audience to an entirely different level of advertising. This translates into successful sales figures which are what advertising is all about. It also motivates and puts the target audience in touch with what is important to them.

Scientific research has as well demonstrated the significant increase in value of anything when it's visually exposed to a targeted audience. This, in a certain way, is instantly taken to a totally different level with video, which indirectly produces the perception of a higher value for the products and/or services being offered to the viewers.

Video marketing speaks to a person the way no other form of advertising has managed to. Video marketing is able to produce the perceived want and need in a person for something they may not even know about, or pay attention to, until being exposed to this sort of marketing approach.

What Works For Marketing

Each business strategist needs to be aware of the most current, viable and successful ways of earning and maintaining optimal business success. Comprehending the fact that marketing has made a shift form a one-way broadcast to a multi-point conversation is a great start. Nowadays, a huge number of consumers utilize online searches when looking to research products and services.

Types of Video for Marketing

Video marketing has fast become an increasingly popular tool used to get hold of a wider target audience. Individuals seek out these forms of marketing and advertising tools to help them discover answers to their questions, show them how to accomplish something or when they would like to read about reviews on a particular product, service or business.

Therefore, considering the utilization of video marketing for local businesses will introduce the most potent way of reaching a target audience by way of data provided, education about products and services, building a community of users and more. Currently, more and more individuals are making a buying decision based on a specific video marketing tool they've come in contact with. In fact, several search engines have noted an increased interest in likely buyers seeking information on services and/or product through online facilities, one of which is video marketing.

It's true that video marketing is the new wave in online marketing, and particularly for local business marketing. However, it's also true that it has to be done correctly in order to prove effective. As with any other technique of promotion, it's crucial to tap the right nerves of the receivers so that they consider buying.

The following are among the most effective kinds of videos you can make:

1. Videos that go into detail describing products and services. These short videos speak concisely about particular products and services and are built more like PowerPoint presentations where the

features and benefits are detailed and discussed in a bullet format so that the viewer may comprehend them easily.

For your business promotion, you may utilize the video to explain the concept of the business telling individuals mostly what they'll have to do and what they'll get in return. Additionally, assorted statistical points, such as individuals who are already progressing with the network and making great incomes, may be a part of the presentation videos.

2. Videos reviewing products and services. These tend to be more elusive videos, but they do work for certain types of businesses. For instance, you may get a third party to review your business in a matter-of-fact manner.

    These videos have a huge impact as those watching the videos think that your business is big enough to merit a review. Reviews always help for branding, whether they're positive or negative. You'll get a brand built up, and naturally, most reviewers will highlight the favorable points. Some marketing entrepreneurs have even been known to hire individuals to do reviews for them in the form of video presentations.

3. Videos giving instructions. These videos are typically designed like tutorials. They're helpful to the end user in a lot of ways as they show them how the product or service works as well as giving detailed instructions for using the product or service if need be. Videos of this nature have the greatest possibility of being bookmarked; basically meaning individuals who have watched them once will keep watching them again and again.

4. Headshot videos. These videos work for promotion and for adding to your own publicity. You speak about the product or service of your choice and the video captures you as you're talking. The effect here is that the viewer knows that you are a real flesh-and-blood person, capable of emotions and expressions. This builds a feeling of trust which may increase the likelihood of them wanting to do business with you.

As can clearly be seen, there are assorted kinds of videos being used for promotion. Consider which style will be best for your business and go ahead with one, or more, of them.

6 Steps to Effective Video Marketing

Video marketing is exceptional because it has the power to grow virally. Viral marketing means it spreads as fast, and as widely, as a biological virus, only in the marketing sense. This may help you reach a wide audience in a short amount of time and at a humble cost.

Have a Look

People love watching videos so much more because of the visual and audio elements you use, which may excite emotions and make the material interesting. Ebooks are so yesterday and have a hard time keeping up with videos, which have been getting better and better as time goes on.

Why are they called video sharing sites? It's because everybody who uploads videos is like a TV channel of their own and those videos are then shared with potentially millions of others. You may get subscribers and individuals who watch your videos freely share it with others through a wide assortment of social media sharing tools that are readily made available.

Among the most useful sites out there is YouTube - The world's largest video sharing site. The popularity of YouTube has exploded over the last few years. Businesses, big and small, stand a lot to gain by tapping into this phenomenon. YouTube lets you upload videos for free, and if your videos meet their standards they'll even offer you a director's status, where you can post up videos longer than 10 minutes.

One good thing about YouTube is that you may post descriptions down at the bottom of your videos in a specially designated box. This lets you draw traffic to your site by just writing descriptions about your videos.

YouTube also has the distinct advantage of being owned by Google, the largest search engine in the world. Because of that, YouTube's videos rank highly on Google, and you may draw plenty of traffic by targeting keywords with a high search volume that are related to your business.

Here's how you begin marketing your business utilizing YouTube:

1. Produce a video of valuable materials related to your business type.

2. Make certain there's a call to action at the end of the video.

3. Upload your video to YouTube.

4. Add a description below every video.

5. Make sure to include a link to your site (traffic drawing purposes).

6. Share your videos with your target audience.

Remember, a really important part of video marketing is the sharing component. Get your subscribers and followers to portion out your videos with others to get more views. The more views you acquire, the higher your video will be ranked. Videos with higher rank will commonly be featured in YouTube's channel listings, and this will further increase your video's views.

Let's look into some easy tools for producing videos for marketing purposes. Among my favorite combinations are Microsoft PowerPoint + Camstasia.

Microsoft PowerPoint lets you produce video content through slides, animations and sound effects. Camstasia lets you record a screen capture, so when you play your slides in real time, you may record every single thing that's occurring. Camstasia also lets you edit your videos with basic features like audio editing, slide transitions and more. Post video production is followed by uploading to YouTube, which is done instantly via Camstasia.

When combined with some cool music, you may make powerful enlightening videos which your client base will love. Of course, you'll need to sign up for a YouTube account before you may begin uploading videos.

In short, these tools will help you produce simple yet powerful videos for acquiring traffic and customers, as long as you have good material that your target market will enjoy. With video marketing, the sky is really the limit.

ESSENTIAL TIPS FOR SOCIAL MEDIA MARKETING

How To Use Social Media To Grow Your Chiropractic Firm Fast!

200 tips from the pros to help you use social media effectively in marketing your business. How to create and optimize your social media profiles, what to share, when and where to share it, and how to build your online social presence so your prospective customers know, like, and trust you… then recommend you to their contacts.

The Big Reference Guide of Social Media Marketing Tips

Social media sites like Facebook and Twitter present an excellent online marketing opportunity, opening new possibilities for communication and improving how people connect and share. Think of social media as an online playground, where people can meet and interact electronically.

As you know, business thrives where there are people. Realizing how many people log into social media sites on a daily basis, Internet marketers have found a new marketing channel for their online businesses.

It used to be that social media sites were just an ingenious way for people to meet up, connect and share. Today, they are one of the most powerful advertising tools business owners can use to connect to their target market.

However, social media marketing is like a double-edged sword – it is something that needs to be wielded carefully and correctly. In the hands of a skilled marketer, it is an effective sales tool. In the hands of an amateur, it can turn success into disaster.

To help you avoid the pitfalls of social media marketing, we have compiled a list of 200 tips designed to guide you to the proper use of social media sites. Read on and learn how you can turn social media sites into an effective marketing tool for your business.

Tips on choosing your first social media site to use

- <u>Choose a social media site that is popular in your area</u>. Of course, you want people to view your social media site; the goal is to attract people in your target market. However, there are social media sites that are popular in some countries, but not in others. For instance, it appears that Facebook is more widely used in Asian countries while Western countries are more likely to be active on Twitter.

- <u>Consider using multiple social media sites.</u> If people in your target market routinely use multiple social media sites, it would be wise to create an account with all of these sites. This way, you will be able to reach more of your target market.

Tips on getting started with a social media site

- <u>Plan your content first.</u> Getting started without a plan can lead to disastrous results, which will not be good for your company's image. Before you make your social media account visible, make sure you thoroughly plan your content and design first.

- <u>Create an editorial calendar.</u> You may have plenty of things you want to share and say. This is great, but if you post everything at the same time, people will get confused, and you will quickly run out of things to share. Instead, make a timeline and plan what you want to post and when you want to post it.

- <u>Know your target market.</u> There are plenty of people who join social media sites. However, your goal is not to reach out to all of them. You need to focus on the group of people who are potential customers. Learn and know who these people are.

- <u>Check for existing accounts with names similar to yours.</u> You don't want people to confuse you for another organization, group or individual. You don't know how these other accounts are behaving or are perceived, and anything they do might have implications on your company's image.

- Use checkusernames.com to create a unique moniker. If you discover there are already existing accounts with names similar to yours, use checkusernames.com to help brainstorm and come up with an alternative name.

- Know how to lure your target market niche in. Do you already have a clear vision of your target market? Once you do, you need to figure out how you can lure them in, which will include conducting research regarding what interests them. For example, if you sell cosmetics and your target market is women, perhaps some video content about makeup tricks will attract them.

- Use high quality graphics and Photoshop edited photos. Sometimes, it is not the content but the appearance that lures visitors. What really draws some people into a social media profile is its appearance. Make your profile page look more attractive by using high quality pictures, photographs and images.

- Use high quality short articles, comments and posts. After being lured in by your attractive graphics and page design, your visitors will start looking for content. If they find nothing, they will leave. For some juicy content, you can outsource the creation of short articles, comments and posts.

- Make sure you have the resources to maintain a social media account regularly. While it is free to sign up to use Facebook and Twitter, you may need to hire graphics artists, video editors, content writers and a profile maintenance crew. If you need to advertise, you will need to budget for ad spots on these social media sites.

- Determine whether having a social media account will really help your company, or if it will just be a liability. There are a lot of benefits to having a social media account for your company, but there can also dangers. You need to analyze whether you are prepared to take on these potential risks.

- <u>Know the dangers and risks of having a social media account</u> and determine whether the risks are worth it or not.

Tips on keeping subscribers glued to your account

- <u>Keep your pages looking beautiful and professional.</u> You may need to hire people to do this for you. This is important because if your social media profile looks shabby, people will probably not come away with a very good impression of your company.

- <u>Sport a page design that corresponds to the nature of your company.</u> You can't just decide on what design to use based on your personal taste. Instead, it needs to be based on the nature of your products and services. For example, if your products are for children, your page should look fun and colorful.

- <u>Post new comments and news regularly.</u> If you do not post regularly, your subscribers will think your company is simply not active. To avoid this perception, you need to post news and comments on a regular basis.

- <u>Always respond to questions if possible.</u> Avoid ignoring your subscribers. People will certainly ask questions, and you should provide a timely response if you can. This is one way to show hospitality, which people tend to appreciate.

- <u>Don't only use words. Use multimedia once in a while.</u> If all your announcements are always simple text, they will soon get boring for viewers no matter how interesting your posts are. Once in a while, try to convey what you want to say through a variety of videos, images and presentations.

- <u>Try sporting different design schemes from time to time.</u> Sticking to one design theme throughout the entire year can be rather boring. It may also give people the impression that you lack resources, so try sporting a new look for your page from time to time. One good tip is to follow the change of seasons (a summer look, a winter look and so on) or you can sync with upcoming holidays (a Christmas look, a Halloween look and so on).

- <u>A logo is not enough. Upload photos related to your company.</u> Some companies only upload their company logo, which is boring. Mix it up by posting photos of your business in action, your employees, your customers, and more.

- <u>Upload photos of recent events that involve your company.</u> If your company hosts or attends an event, you should post photographs of it. This way, people will see that your company is active.

- <u>Do poll questions once in a while to keep it exciting.</u> Studies show that people like answering quick poll questions on social media sites. Try taking a poll once in a while to entertain your subscribers. Be sure keep it related to your business. For example, if you are in the fashion industry, maybe do a poll of which among a list of artists is more fashionable.

- <u>Post updates about new promos your company offers.</u> Your social media profiles are a great channel you can use to announce promos and events your company hosts. When done regularly, it will keep your subscribers checking your profile.

Tips on using multimedia content

- <u>Use only high quality media content.</u> Do not settle for mediocre quality. The quality of the media content you upload will have a huge impact on your company's image. Make sure you only use high quality content to ensure a positive impact.

- <u>Instead of uploading videos to an actual social media account, consider using links instead.</u> Some social media sites limit the size of the files you can upload. Instead of trying to upload a video that is too large to a blog site, consider uploading it to YouTube first and then link or embed the YouTube URL to your blog site.

- <u>Choose multimedia designs that suit your target market.</u> The design scheme of any multimedia content you upload should match the nature of your business.

- <u>Always proofread for grammatical or spelling mistakes, and check facts and links before uploading so as to maintain credibility.</u> If you outsource your video or graphic needs, check all content for errors first before you upload anything.

- <u>Know the upload limitations of your social media of choice.</u> Facebook, for example, limits how many megabytes you can upload per file. Learn these limits so you can plan which multimedia files you can use on which site.

- <u>Remove old multimedia uploads to free up your upload capacity.</u> If you run out of storage space and need to upload a new file, look at previously uploaded media files you may no longer need. Delete them to create extra storage space.

- <u>Know which uploads should never be removed, no matter what.</u> Not all multimedia you previously uploaded should be removed. Some of it needs to stay for your subscribers to see. For example, if you uploaded a video that features the product specs of your main product, you should probably always keep that video file for any new subscribers to see.

- <u>HD quality is good, but do not always use it.</u> Your subscribers will certainly appreciate an HD quality video upload. However, these high quality videos tend to take up a lot of space. Even if you use YouTube, an HD file will take longer to load, especially on slower connections.

- <u>The dimension of photographs does not always have to be big in order to be high quality.</u> There is a fallacy that the higher the pixels a photo is, the better the photo quality and clarity. Truth be told, this is not always the case. It all depends on the editing and a 640x480 photo could look clearer than a 1024x720 photo.

Tips on using language

- <u>Decide on a language to use.</u> English may be considered the international language, but you need to consider your target market before choosing English automatically. If your target market speaks another language, you might want to consider using that as your primary language.

- <u>Consider duplicate pages that are translated to other languages.</u> If you are targeting a market niche that is composed of people from different countries and ethnicities, you may wish to consider several accounts that each utilize a specific language.

- <u>Use the appropriate tone and language to suit your targeted market niche.</u> For children's toys, you should sound fun. For fashion items, you should sound trendy. For serious stuff, you should sound corporate.

- <u>Be precise and brief in your message.</u> People dislike reading lengthy, drawn out messages. As a general rule, people are busy, so keep you posts and comments brief and concise.

- <u>Always double check spelling and grammar before posting.</u> Grammatical errors and typos can quickly tarnish your company image. Poor grammar and multiple spelling errors can lead people to think your posts are done in a hurry and with no regard for quality.

Tips on using YouTube effectively

- <u>Decide on the appropriate comment sharing settings for your YouTube account.</u> You can block certain users from posting comments on your videos and on your profile page. Do this to prevent possible derogatory comments.

- <u>Decide on whether to allow use of the "Like" and "Dislike" buttons or not.</u> Dislikes can have a negative effect on potential customers. If you think your video might possibly get a lot of dislikes, you can always turn this option off.

- Learn how to use related tags. If you want people find your uploaded video on YouTube easily, you should use tags which are likely to be used when typing keywords in the search bar. Computer products, for examples, might do well with tags such as iPad, laptop, Internet and Microsoft.

- Check comments regularly. If you decided to allow comments, you should check them regularly so you can deal with derogatory and damaging comments as soon as possible.

- Use the "delete comment" option sparingly. On YouTube, a comment can never completely be removed. The username of the person who posted the comment will still be there with the note "deleted comment." This can make people wonder why you deleted a comment so this option should be used sparingly.

- Use courteous and well-informed replies instead of deleting. Instead of deleting a negative comment, you can carefully reply to the derogatory messages instead. Don't be rude, but simply make your point in a very convincing and informed manner so readers will side with you because of the way you answered.

- Customize your page and use your logo for better credibility. Using a company logo adds credibility. This helps the customization on your page, making it look more authentic.

- Upload only high quality videos. Videos do not have to be in HD to be high quality and clear; however they do need to be properly done and edited. All videos should be high quality for the sake of your company's image.

- Screen videos for possibly offensive elements. People on YouTube can be pretty harsh, so make sure that all the videos you upload are free of potentially offensive content.

- Take time to learn YouTube's policies. It can be very damaging to the reputation of your company if your account gets suspended as people will wonder why it happened. So, take time to read YouTube's policies in order to avoid suspension.

- <u>Announce key user increases to your subscribers.</u> Always update your first 1000, 5000, 10,000, 100,000, and so on, subscribers. Make these announcements so your subscribers can see your page is moving forward.

Tips on how to expand the reach of your social media account

- <u>Advertise your social media account.</u> The purpose of your social media account is to advertise. However, a social media account is an advertisement tool that also needs to be advertised. So, conduct some self advertising by telling people to visit your social media account.

- <u>Always include your social media URL in your other forms of advertisement.</u> If you advertise in magazines, on television or radio, make sure your social media account is mentioned. Saying "Like us on Facebook" should be sufficient.

- <u>Learn to use SEO techniques.</u> When making posts and uploading articles to your blog make sure they are created with SEO in mind. This will make your social media account easier for your target market to find through the various search engines.

- <u>Contribute SEO articles to websites like</u> www.ezinearticles.com. By contributing quality SEO articles to these types of article submission sites, you make your social media page easier to find.

- <u>Use a URL that corresponds to the main keyword which best describes the products and services offered by your company.</u> You can change how your URL appears. For example, if your company name is Solemn Foods, you can change your Facebook URL to www.facebook.com/solemnfoods

- <u>Get affiliated with other groups related to your market niche.</u> By becoming affiliates of other groups related to your field, you expose your social media profile page to more potential viewers. For example, if you are selling cosmetics, you should probably become affiliated with multiple pages about makeup tutorials, makeup tips, the latest makeup trends and more.

- Use "follow" and "like" buttons. These are buttons which you can post elsewhere on the Internet. This way, users can follow and like the content you post on your Facebook account, without actually logging in to Facebook or opening another window.

- Make use of affiliates and links. Have affiliate sites post a link that will direct visitors to your blog site. This is one reason it is important to have many affiliates on the Internet. It will help you gain more subscribers.

- Make use of the old school method of email marketing. Yes, it is old, but it is still effective. Send potential leads an email that contains a link and a follow button that will connect them to your blog.

- Propose a guest post on established and influential blogs – ideally the big names in your niche. Ask other influential groups to allow you to make a post on their page. On that post, make sure to include a link that will direct readers to your blog.

- Your subscription buttons should be done via RSS. Using RSS will allow users to see the latest updates on your blog.

Tips on outsourcing work and tasks

- Make sure the outsourcer you hire knows your ideals and standards. If you choose to hire a person to manage and maintain your blog page they should know your standards. They need to understand how you want to run things to ensure a smooth operation.

- Have someone check the site throughout the day and night. You never know when a user might have posted something derogatory on your page. Therefore, it is important that you have someone check your blog page from time to time, both day and night, to filter out any such negative comments.

- Set limits on how much an outsourcer can change. Outsourcers you hire to manage your blog page should have limitations. There are things that they should not touch or change. Be clear and upfront about this.

- <u>Delegate different tasks to different people if necessary.</u> For better results, you can delegate someone to manage events, promos, news, and so on. Then, you could hire another person for articles, videos, graphics and the page design.

- <u>You can hire people to do the graphics.</u> Photoshop is not easy. If you are looking for professional results, hire someone to do the work for you.

- <u>You can hire people to create videos.</u> There are several video maker software programs available today. If you are not confident with video creation, do not attempt to make your own as it will only lead to low quality output. When in doubt about video production, outsource the work to a professional.

- <u>You can hire people to create short articles.</u> This is now easy to find. You can hire ghost writers to write articles and even eBooks for you.

Tips on dealing with trolling, defamation and derogatory comments from users

- <u>Check for possible derogatory messages all the time.</u> Check your page frequently for any comments that carry a negative tone, or at least have someone do it for you. You need to deal with negative comments as soon as possible before they affect the opinion of other subscribers.

- <u>Avoid the domino effect of negative comments.</u> When one person makes a negative comment, it is possible that others will sympathize. Then it can become a string of negative comments from more users. Stop this before this happens by addressing the root cause.

- <u>Do not leave a serious question hanging unanswered for too long.</u> Some questions, if unanswered, can lead users to doubt your company's credibility (e.g. The product I bought has lasted only a month, can I have it replaced?). Questions like this one should be answered immediately to show your company's attentiveness.

- Maintain a professional tone when replying to derogatory comments. Sometimes, you need to answer derogatory questions to set things straight, so other users will know the truth. Though it may be tempting, you should avoid being defensive and don't get rude. You should always maintain a professional tone. Other users will see this and appreciate your professionalism.

- Know which messages should be left unanswered. You do not need to respond to every question.

Tips on using Facebook

- Open a business/group account, rather than using your personal account. There are two types of account you can open on Facebook. For social media marketing, you should open a group account instead of a personal account. Its features are designed for marketing.

- Get your first 25 likes as soon as possible. A group account will only have access to all the programming and professional features once it gathers 25 likes from other users.

- Consider using the paid advertisement service from Facebook. Facebook offers a tool that will make your page appear on the advertisement section of other Facebook users. With this paid option, you can even set your advertisements to appear only for a select market niche (age filter, address filter, gender filter, etc.).

- Post what your subscribers will want to share. If one of your subscribers shares a post from your page, it will be available in their profile page. This way, it will be exposed to everyone on the friend list of that person. This will extend the reach of your social media account in a big way.

- <u>Like pages or groups which are in some way connected to your market niche.</u> By liking pages from other Facebook groups, you are increasing your exposure to the subscribers of those pages.

- <u>Like pages or groups that are frequented by your target customers.</u> Go to pages which your target customers might frequent. For example, if your target customers are women, you might find them frequenting fashion pages. Like those pages and perhaps post a comment to those pages to help them find you.

- <u>Get help from people you know who also have Facebook accounts.</u> Getting started on Facebook can sometimes be the difficult part. Remember, it's okay to ask for help at first. Ask people you know to like your page and ask them to share the contents of your page. Their friends might just help out as a direct result.

- <u>Include a photo album that shows the faces of your company's staff members. Studies</u> show that people trust online organizations more if they can see faces. If there is no face, it is as if the organization is hiding something. People like to have a face to put with a name.

- <u>Keep photo albums organized according to an event or date.</u> People like to browse photos. But, it can be annoying if different photos are just mixed together with no rhyme or reason. Make sure you organize all your photos in albums according to specific events and/or dates.

- <u>Advertise your Facebook account on your other social media accounts.</u> If you have a Twitter account, for example, send out a Tweet inviting your followers to check out your Facebook page.

- <u>Use only one account per social media site, in most cases.</u> This is to prevent confusion. If your products and services are not widely varied, then there is no reason to have more than one Facebook account.

- <u>Use several accounts only if your company has varied sectors.</u> For example, if your company sells different products (e.g. clothes, food, toys), you might want to consider separate accounts or pages for each individual product line.

- Use your Facebook account to connect with people you meet on business trips and meetings. Meeting potential affiliates in meetings and while on business trips is always a possibility. Use your company's Facebook account to stay connected.

- Your Facebook posts should be in harmony with your Twitter posts. Contradicting posts on your Twitter and Facebook accounts can be seen as inconsistent. Subscribers might question how your company runs things if you are saying one thing on one account and the polar opposite on the other.

- Update significant increases in subscribers. Let people know that your number of subscribers is growing especially when the increase is significant. This will give a positive impression and show that your company is moving forward.

Tips on using Twitter

- Edit your Twitter URL name, using a main keyword which best describes your company. From the default URL assigned to your profile by Twitter, edit it into something like www.twitter.com/YouCompanyNameHere.

- Regularly Tweet news and events. If you leave your Twitter account unattended, people will stop following you or un-follow you altogether. Even if they don't un-follow you, they might stop checking your Tweets.

- Follow groups, organizations, companies and/or people you believe are connected to your company in some way. Follow Twitter users that are related to the nature of your business. This will increase your exposure to a greater number of Twitter users.

- Avoid posting Tweets on other's profiles. This is to maintain a professional attitude. Remember, this is a company account not a personal account.

- <u>Avoid using your company Twitter account for personal use.</u> If you like a certain celebrity or you like to make comments about some current events that are completely unrelated to your business, you should do so using a personal Twitter account. Business and personal life should not be mixed on your company's Twitter account.

- <u>Avoid conveying personal feelings and thoughts via your company Twitter account.</u> Tweets about your bath time, your breakfast, the new clothes you bought and your quarrel with your friends do not belong in your company's Twitter account.

- <u>Advertise your Twitter account on your other social media accounts.</u> If you have a Facebook account, tell your Facebook subscribers that you also have a Twitter account. This way, both accounts have the chance to gain more subscribers.

- <u>Hashtags (#) are not very effective.</u> A recent study shows that posts using hashtags are actually 5% less efficient at attracting users.

- <u>Do not follow more people than the number of people following you.</u> If you are following more people than the number of people following you, it can make you look desperate, which is not good for your company image.

- <u>Use the geo-location feature to help find your local target niche.</u> This feature is very useful for Internet marketing as it will help you locate your target customers easier and faster.

- <u>Focus more on your advocates than your influencers.</u> Your influencers are likely to mention you only once or twice after which, you are not really connected with them. However, advocates are different. Advocates are potentially long-term partners with long-term benefits, so your time is better spent when invested with them.

- <u>Your Tweets should be in harmony with your Facebook posts.</u> Make sure that company news, events, and promos you Tweet are the same with those you post on your Facebook account. Consistency is important for image.

- Update users about any significant increase in followers.

Tips for safety

- Be transparent while exercising caution. Your subscribers will like it if you are transparent and limit how much information you withhold. This allows them to feel more connected with you.

- Only display your company's personal addresses. You are not obliged, nor is it safe, to tell your subscribers your personal address or the personal address of your employees. Only tell them the address of your actual company.

- Only display your company's contact number, email, fax, etc. Only company contact information should be displayed for users to see. Any personal contact information, including that of your employees, should not be disclosed to protect privacy.

- Avoid heated exchanges. Not only is it unprofessional, but it will only leave your followers with a negative taste in their mouths.

- Keep a record of possibly threatening comments. If a comment you receive includes anything threatening, you should be sure keep a record of it, such as a screen capture.

- Never use a password that is easy to guess. You don't know what hackers might do to your social media accounts, so it's better to fend them off from the start. The best way to do this is by selecting a password that can't be guessed easily.

- Always withhold the email address that is used to register a social media account. This may all be that a hacker needs to hack into your Facebook or Twitter account. It should be kept private at all times to avoid such a disaster.

- <u>Use a registration email that is different from your company email.</u> <u>Hackers</u> typically attempt to use the official company email thinking that it was used to open a company's Facebook or Twitter account. Therefore, set up a special email specifically for registering all your social media accounts.

- <u>Never leave any account unattended on your computer.</u> Don't forget to uncheck the "Keep Me Logged In" button. Some people forget to uncheck this box. As a result, their account can easily hacked by the next person to use the computer.

- <u>Avoid logging in on public computers.</u> Even if you uncheck the Keep Me Logged In button, there are still ways for hackers to get your username and password. A simple keylogger program will do the trick. If you must login using a public computer or a public network, try using the onscreen QWERTY board when keying in the username and password.

- <u>Keylogger programs follow the keystrokes that you make.</u> They can't read passwords and usernames that are input using an onscreen qwerty keyboard. The downside is that people behind you will be able to see which characters you are clicking, so keep that in mind.

- <u>Change your password</u> if you believe it has been compromised.

- <u>Remove arguments between users.</u> Sometimes, a dispute may not be between you and a user but among users themselves. Remove these as soon as possible and block them if necessary.

- <u>Create a Rules and Conditions page.</u> Some people may not read this verbiage, but if they violate your terms, you can then ban them and they will not be able to say that they were not warned.

Tips on what you should avoid

- <u>Avoid "liking", "following" or getting linked in any way to celebrities.</u> This is part of professionalism. Business is business and involvement with Hollywood seems like a personal matter. The only exception is if a certain celebrity is somehow linked to your business.

- <u>116. Avoid "liking", "following" or getting linked in any way to politicians.</u> People are always divided with their political views. You could lose possible customers if you favor politicians and political decisions which they do not approve of.

- <u>Avoid voicing opinions on controversial matters.</u> Besides politics, there are other controversial issues that can divide the opinion of people. Avoid making statements about such matters.

- <u>Avoid using your company's social media accounts to post comments that convey your personal feelings and thoughts.</u> You may have strong opinions about current events, but you should avoid making them on your company's social media account.

- <u>Avoid uploading content that is not related to your market, unless it is part of your marketing strategy.</u> Sometimes, it may be necessary to add some fun "fluff" as a form of entertainment, just be sure you do not make it a habit.

- <u>Avoid media content that is potentially offensive to any group or people.</u> Racism is especially a sensitive topic. Avoid making any potentially offensive comment, even a practical joke, because some people may take offense to the statement.

- <u>Avoid jokes,</u> unless they are completely inoffensive.

Tips on maintaining/improving the credibility of your social media account

- <u>If your company has an official webpage, make sure to mention your social media account on it.</u> This is one way of encouraging people to subscribe to your social media account. If you get them to subscribe to you, you are also gaining access to the people in their friends list.

- <u>Don't forget to use your company logo</u> on your social media accounts.

- <u>Post photos of company events – the kinds which the public could not possibly get access to otherwise.</u> Random photos like dinners, tours and even photos in airports are the kinds of photos that others could not normally have access to. Using this method, people know that your social media account is authentic and your subscribers will feel like they have priority access to you.

- <u>Make sure your social media announcements correspond to the announcements on your official webpage.</u> If you are also making announcements on your official webpage, they should contain the same details that the announcements you make on your social media accounts do.

- <u>Be careful about making statements about current events.</u> Avoid it altogether if possible. People have different opinions about current events. If you favor one side, you might incite the anger of others.

- <u>Always give your subscribers the feeling that the company is moving forward.</u> People will tend to trust your company more if they believe that your company is moving forward. Always strive give this impression through the posts that you make.

- <u>Always give your subscribers the feeling that your company's social media account pages are active and kicking.</u>

- <u>When mistakes happen, step up and own them.</u> Even with a lot of precaution, it is possible that a mistake or two will occur. If this happens, just admit your mistake and apologize.

- <u>Act like a leader, without being arrogant.</u> People need to feel that you are a leader – a driving force. If you do this without being arrogant, they will respect you.

- <u>Always post media exposure of your company.</u> If your company has been featured in a magazine, a television show or on any media channel, make sure that you mention it on your social media sites. Provide a link to the story if available.

Tips on measuring and improving the effectiveness of your social media

- <u>Analyze how many of your customers came to you through your social media accounts.</u> Conduct polls and surveys to know how many of your customers learned about your company through your social media accounts. This way, you will know if your social media venture is fruitful or not.

- <u>Blog regularly for better traffic.</u> Making blog posts on a regular basis will keep people tuned into your page and will increase traffic. After all, why regularly check a page that rarely makes blog posts?

- <u>Imagine that social media is like a story that you tell</u>, and the characters in the story are your customers.

- <u>Don't just talk about your company.</u> Interact and talk about the people who subscribe to your accounts. If you speak about your subscribers and customers as well, they will feel important and involved. This will help you improve your relationship with them.

- <u>Use polls so you learn more about your customers.</u> Polls let you know the preferences of your subscribers. This can help generate ideas for your marketing game plan.

- <u>Try other smaller scale social media sites for localized marketing.</u> If there is a local social media site in the area of your targeted market niche, consider opening an account there. This will help you reach out to more locals.

- <u>Offer a mobile check-in feature if it is compatible with your business.</u> It is now getting popular for businesses to allow their customers to order and/or check-in for services and/or products online. Offer this feature to open up your services to more customers.

Tips on coming up with good content

- Always stay updated on current events. Current events may give you ideas about the future of your market. Stay updated so you are not left behind in any market changes.

- Check the latest news in your business sector. You always need to check for current events, but you need to focus more on news that involves your market niche and your business sector. Make posts about these news events as long as you do not side with any specific group.

- Regularly check the Yahoo! Homepage. The homepage of Yahoo! is a great place to find some of the juiciest and latest news. They even often feature business news regularly.

- Regularly read magazines that are related to your field. Magazines can give you a lot of ideas. For example, if your business is about fashion, then you should read a lot of fashion magazines.

- Hire researchers if possible. Research is not always an easy task, especially if it involves marketing and business. If you do not have extra time for conducting research, you can hire others to do it for you.

- Think "out of the box" and come up with something unique. Try going out of your comfort zone once in a while. Think of new and exciting ways to make your announcements and posts so your subscribers don't get bored.

- If you need to recycle content, make sure to present it in a way that is fresh. Sometimes, you just really run out of new content. While recycling content is discouraged, sometimes it is necessary. If you must do this, make sure you make it look new and different.

- <u>Ask your customers and subscribers what they want to see next.</u> If you have no idea what your subscribers might like to see next, you can simplify things by asking them. In fact, customers like it when you ask questions like, "What do you want to see next?" or "What do you want us to make for you next?"

- <u>Ask your affiliates what they want you to do next.</u> Don't just ask your customers and subscribers what they want to see next. Never forget about your affiliates, advocates, and influencers and ask them as well.

- <u>Check your previous contents and see what might be missing.</u> You might think that you have already done almost everything. But check your profile again. You never know what you might discover is missing.

Tips on writing powerful comments and posts

- <u>Come up with a good title.</u> Sometimes, subscribers won't even try to read if they see that a post is lengthy. So what should you do? Incite their interest by starting your post with a catchy and intriguing title.

- <u>Always use a catchy headline.</u> If a title isn't a good fit for the post, simply start with a catchy and interesting first sentence.

- <u>Use the inverted triangle method of writing.</u> This means that you should write your articles by including all the important information in the beginning of the article. The concentration of information is higher in the beginning and gets less as the article ends.

Tips on unique ways to deliver your message

- <u>Use PowerPoint presentations.</u> Tired of old-school paragraph posts? Then create a powerful presentation instead and add some exciting designs and animations.

- <u>Use images.</u> You can also use graphic art to tell your story by using images.

- <u>Use video clips.</u> This is just like doing a PowerPoint presentation.

- <u>Use voice clips.</u> Try something new once in a while and convey your message through recorded voice. This is actually a more effective marketing strategy because a voice can be far more engaging than plain written words.

- <u>Combine all of the above.</u> All the tricks used above can be used at the same time. This will make for a unique and effective way of communicating with your subscribers.

- <u>Use lists and bullet points.</u> A long paragraph is tiring to read. Make it easier for your subscribers to read by making a list.

- <u>Use all uppercase letters on important words.</u> This is one way to entice your subscribers to read a rather boring- looking paragraph. Highlight words like BONUS, SALE, PROMO and such. Keywords like these in all caps will surely catch their attention.

- <u>Use double quotations as necessary.</u> Like using all caps, this is another effective way to highlight an important word.

- <u>Use underlines as necessary.</u> Underlines are also an effective highlighting element.

- <u>Use highlighting if your social media account allows.</u> Adding a colored highlight to a word will make it stand out more than all caps, a double quote or an underline. Not all social media sites offer this option.

- <u>Know the proper use of the opening word "ATTENTION!"</u> Sometimes you can simply start a paragraph with "ATTENTION!" Use this sparingly and make sure the message is really worth opening.

- <u>Occasional humor is okay.</u> Professionalism should be observed at all times, but some humor will put a smile on the face of your readers. If they are happy, they are more likely to buy.

- <u>Subscribe</u> to newsletters of affiliates.

- <u>Subscribe</u> to newsletters of similar groups.

- <u>Subscribe</u> to newsletters of competitors.

Tips on improving customer relationships

- <u>Write about the success stories of your customers.</u> Feature examples of some of your customers who liked your products and services. This will entice others to try your products and services for themselves.

- <u>Post how-to guides for your subscribers.</u> It has been proven in Internet marketing that most people like reading how-to-guides. If you provide some once in a while, people will keep coming back to check your page.

- <u>Include guides about mistakes to avoid.</u> This way, your customers and subscribers will feel that you actually care about their well-being. This will be good for your business as long as the guides are related to your market niche.

- <u>Post interviews with successful clients.</u> Don't just tell stories about a successful customer and/or client. Instead, post a video of an interview. This is a lot more convincing that just plain text.

- <u>Avoid recycling previous messages.</u> You may have no choice but to recycle content in some instances. But, avoid it if at all possible, especially with messages. Some users will still notice that content is recycled even after a lot of editing and changes.

- <u>Avoid recycling multimedia elements.</u> Multimedia content can also be recycled. But, do so only when you have no choice and edit the content so it is not recognized as a recycled item.

- <u>Send out important newsletters to subscribers.</u> Sometimes, subscribers just stop checking out your page, and it's not even your fault. Maybe they just got busy for a period of time and forgot. Whatever the case may be, it helps to remind them that you are still there through newsletters.

- <u>Always use courteous greetings, daily if possible.</u> On days when you have nothing to say, a simple "Good morning" and "Good evening" or "Happy lunch time" will do. You can also use greetings as an opening to any announcement.

- <u>Make sure your subscribers feel that they are always up-to-date.</u> This is one of the advantages of making announcements and posting news regularly. This ensures subscribers feel they are not left out of the latest happenings with your company.

- <u>Talk about the latest trends</u> which you know your subscribers will want to hear about.

Tips on dealing with competition

- <u>Check the social media site of your competitors regularly.</u> Who knows, your competitors might have come up with a cool new way to present ideas. Looking at the page of your competitors will give you more ideas, which you can use together with your own original ideas.

- <u>Check the official homepages of your competitors.</u> You can also take a look at the official webpages of your competitors to see how they are advertising their social media accounts.

- <u>Subscribe to the newsletters of your competitors.</u> Use your personal account for this. You can subscribe to the newsletters of your competitors to see what they are up to. This may also give you new ideas for your own marketing strategies.

- <u>Avoid making negative statements about your competitors.</u> Some may do this to denigrate their competitors. But, this is a dirty trick which many of your subscribers will recognize and simply won't respect.

- If your competitor posts anything against you, avoid getting lured into the trap of answering back. A simple defense on your part to clarify false accusations will do. But, do not return the favor of firing insults back. You want to appear as the good guy, not an argumentative bad guy.

- Avoid posting anything too similar to that of your competitor. Check on your competitors for ideas but don't copy those ideas. Avoid posting anything mockingly similar or using any idea that is exactly the same. Make some changes to it and make it your own.

- Set the trends, don't copy them. Take the lead in your industry. Be a trendsetter, not just a follower.

- Check the number of visits and/or followers your competitors have. This will let you know how well your competitors are doing compared to you and tell you if you need to further enhance your performance.

Tips on financing your social media account

- Some social media only needs to be checked once a day. Checking once daily may be all that your social media account needs. If this is the case, there is no need to pay extra to have it checked several times a day.

- Check your database for currently existing multimedia content. There may be no need to order a new logo or graphics. Check first and see if the ones you used in your previous videos and slideshow might work for your new endeavor.

- Supply currently existing graphics to hired multimedia artists. It might help cut the cost if you provide multimedia artists with your existing graphics and logo.

- <u>Hire freelancers to do smaller tasks.</u> Instead of hiring a regular employee, it is sometimes more cost effective to hire a freelancer to do a smaller task. You can use micro outsourcing, sites like www.microworkers.com, which charges on a per task basis.

- <u>Freelancers from Asian countries are usually more cost effective to hire.</u> Asian freelancers are not necessarily less competent, but they do tend to be less expensive to hire. Many are quite capable of producing world class quality at affordable prices.

- <u>Use safe payment methods.</u> There is no need to dangerously expose your credit card number or your bank account number. Instead, you can use safe payment methods, like PayPal, to protect all your account information.

- <u>Check if there is someone among your employees who can perform a specific task.</u> Maybe there is no need to hire another person to do a specific task. Ask your employees and see if one of them has the skills to perform certain tasks you need to have done.

- <u>Monitor your investment on your social media site is getting returns.</u> Maintaining a social media site will cost money and time. However, if it is not yielding you returns, it may not be an effective marketing strategy for your line of business.

Tips on making your social media account user friendly

- <u>Tell your designer to use a page design that works well on smartphones.</u> Many people check and update their social media accounts regularly via their smartphones. So, it will help if your website is optimized for smartphone viewing.

- <u>Avoid using scripts and content that might run only on the latest software.</u> Some multimedia content requires the latest plug-ins. Such multimedia content might not be viewable to all people and should be avoided if possible.

- <u>Avoid making a page that uploads too slowly. You need a quality page design.</u> However, your page designer must avoid using elements that might take too much time to load. These days, most viewers have a good Internet connection. So, many will not wait for a page that loads too slowly.

- <u>Keep things looking neat and tidy.</u> It doesn't have to be the most stylish but what is important is that your page always looks clean – nothing should be out of place.

- <u>Keep all information organized.</u> Elements and content should be arranged and grouped properly. Have a design that allows your subscribers to easily find what they are looking for.

- <u>Use tabs (if possible) or divisions for different topics.</u> This will allow you to separate different topics and/or discussions and helps keep your content organized without opening multiple social media accounts.

- <u>Avoid complex and confusing words. Just keep it simple.</u> Research shows that most Internet users frown upon complex and confusing words.

- <u>Make your page easy to find.</u> There are many ways to do this. Using SEO and having plenty of backlinks, for example, will make your page easier to find on the Internet. As this is easier said than done, you might find it easier to hire an Internet marketing specialist to do this for you.

Conclusion

This concludes the list of tips for effective social media marketing. But of course, you shouldn't religiously stick to just these rules. Be sensitive to the changes you see and act accordingly.

Be aware of the dangers of social media sites. Take note that many lives have been ruined because of Facebook and/or Twitter. Of course, these sites are not to be blamed. These things happen because of improper use of these social media sites.

CLARENCE WILLIAMS

MOBILE MARKETING MONEY

Mobile Marketing Basics

By using mobile marketing, individual business owners are able to create and execute effective marketing campaigns. This helps ensure direct delivery of their messages to the recipients of their choice within the shortest time possible. Cost is one of the main elements that make mobile marketing very attractive. For example, the cost for text a message is usually nominal when compared to other, more conventional, advertising methods. This all means an increase of volume, but a decrease of cost incurred.

The Basics

Being able to reach a huge target audience fairly quickly is important to the element of effectively delivering the required message. This is important as most other advertising methods are not able to guarantee such a high receiving ratio, or even close to it. The response rate with mobile marketing is typically also much higher when compared to other mediums of advertising.

Mobile marketing also allows individual business owners to design their advertising content to targeted individuals who may be interested in it. This customizing feature is similar to brand messaging. In addition, accessibility is a non-issue as the recipients do not need to be linked to any particular electric equipment, such as computers. This is due to the fact that in order to receive a message, a mobile phone or other mobile device is all that is required. This makes mobile marketing a viable and welcomed option as most individuals today own a mobile phone or other mobile device. Tracking the campaign results is also easier as downloads, page visits, customer opt-ins and many others statistics are immediately visible.

First Build Your List

Having a substantial list of mobile numbers for the purpose of mobile marketing is an important element of mobile marketing, but it may not be the one that guarantees higher revenues. Simply sending random messages to a list of mobile phone numbers is not a guarantee that the parties receiving these messages will respond in the fashion you desire. So, taking the time and effort to build a suitable and effective list, no matter what the size, is much more important than just using one that is lengthy but of no particular benefit to you.

Your List

Building a list of mobile numbers which can be used to effectively market a product or service, must be completed with some thought and focus on the mindset of the target audience. One way of targeting the right people is to design a web form where potential visitors will willingly provide their numbers for the intention of receiving specific information.

This will help ensure a response that will increase the success of your mobile marketing efforts because those on the receiving end of the messages will fit your "target audience" who already have an interest in your particular message content. This also ensures the sender does not send the advertising messages to parties who may view it as a nuisance, or who may have little or no interest in the particular product or service being touted.

As well as online, there are also offline ways in which to build an effective list of mobile phone numbers. For example, the use of business cards helps both parties connect and form an initial contact point for the future exchange of information. Putting some business information on a business card will allow the receiving party to be able to recognize or anticipate a possible message being sent for a mobile marketing purpose. Other methods like newspaper ads, magazine ads or other forms of print ads to gain visibility and build a list are still considered popular by many business owners.

Choose the Right Mobile Campaign

Making the right choice in regards to which mobile campaign is most suitable for a particular product or service is very important as it will largely determine how successful the campaign becomes.

Most campaigns are designed to drive brand awareness, deliver knowledge or elicit a direct response from those receiving the messages. Getting the receiver to understand and gain value from a mobile message is the goal, so choosing the right campaign is vital.

Get the Right One

It's important to keep simplicity and clarity in mind as you develop your mobile campaign. By keeping participation in your mobile campaign simple and straightforward, you will avoid confusing and frustrating message recipients. If your campaign involves a lot of complicated and steps, subscribers will lose interest and ask to be removed from your list.

Having remarketing capabilities within the chosen mobile campaign can also be another advantage. This creates an additional opportunity for the receiving party to respond if they failed to take action on the original opportunity you sent. Just as in any other form of marketing, following up on initial offers often yields more positive results than the original offer. Be consistent and persistent without being annoying, and you are more likely to get the results you desire.

Consider running a mobile campaign that provides virtual rewards. Customers enjoy being rewarded for taking action, and everyone likes free stuff. Further bolster results by choosing a mobile campaign that features interactive elements in the ads. This allows a better response rate as it targets recipients' natural preference for completion of an interaction.

Finally, putting a good tracking system in place is a must. This must-have feature enables you to measure the impact and effectiveness of your campaign. Without this valuable feedback, it's nearly impossible to assess what is and isn't working.

CLARENCE WILLIAMS

SEO PROFITS

How To Generate Free Local Website Traffic Just By Showing Up When People Are Looking For Your Products & Services

Now we will look at what Search Engine Optimization (SEO) is, and the ways in which it can be used. Through this book, we will provide you with the basics on using Search Engine Optimization in order to improve traffic flow to your website.

SEO is considered to be a part of search engine marketing by many people. It is often used when people are describing a process for improving the amount of traffic that flows to a website from various search engines. Many site owners will make use of SEO techniques in an attempt to gain qualified visitors to their site.

The quality of these visitors will often be measured by what specific keywords they are using in order to reach the desired result they want. This might mean they end up making a purchase or it could be that they just end up viewing or downloading a particular page on a particular site. Still other results could be the visitor requesting some further information or signing up for a newsletter.

Search Engine Optimization is a marketing strategy which can often generate a good traffic return for a website. However, what must be remembered is that search engines are not actually paid for the traffic they send to a site from a natural (organic) search. Plus, they will regularly change the algorithms that they use for these searches in an effort to improve the search results for people using their search engine. In fact, there is no guarantee that using this system will be successful in either the long or short term for any website. Because of this, SEO is often compared to traditional forms of PR (Public Relations) while PPC (Pay Per Click) advertising is more closely associated with traditional forms of advertising.

However, even if you do find you have increased traffic to your site because of SEO if your site is unprepared for this influx of traffic, it may in fact be detrimental to your site as visitors will go away feeling dissatisfied. Even worse, they may leave and never return. So, SEO might be considered a marketing tactic with rules all to itself, but many industry experts see beyond this and know it is really part of the bigger picture.

Why Use Search Engine Optimization?

SEO, as already previously mentioned, is a sub-section of search engine marketing. Unfortunately, with SEO, there are no shortcuts, and if you are looking for a way to get quick and easy results, SEO isn't it. Instead, you will need to carry out some hard work to ensure success, especially in relation to the actual content of your site.

SEO, done the right way, can and will see your website placement on the search engines improve, but it won't happen overnight. So, you have to exercise patience and be ever vigilant if you hope to achieve maximum results.

Consider the following points:

Good Content

> This is probably the single most important point you should look at when executing SEO, especially if you want your site to be found easily on the web. Although your site may be technically put together perfectly so that the search engine robots find it, you will quickly discover that it will not help if the actual content of your site is not all that good.

> For the content of your site to be good content, it should be factually and grammatically correct. While it isn't necessary to be perfect, you do have to ensure that the content itself is unique and specific to those who will be finding your page, especially if they are seeking out information specific to your products and/or services.

> Good content leads to more visitors coming back again and again. Many of these visitors will like to your site, which is great for your search engine rankings, especially if they link form a site that has a higher page rank than yours.

> As well as having good content on your site, you also have fresh content. If you add new content to your site on a regular basis, you

are giving your visitors plenty of reasons for returning. Because of this, search engine robots will also visit your site more often as soon as they notice that you are updating it regularly. So, any new content you add will then be indexed much faster in the future.

Check Your Spellings

If your site is written in English, then you're probably aware of the differences in spelling between American and British English. Where in the UK, they will write "colour", in the USA it is written as "color", and the same can be said of "optimization" and "optimization". If you can, why not set up your machine so that the spell checker is set up as USA English rather than British English? Unfortunately, there are many words between these two languages that are often misspelled, and, in fact, the same can be said for many other languages around the world, so check your spelling carefully.

Make Sure Your Page Titles are Descriptive

If you make your page titles as simple, descriptive and relevant as possible, it will make it easier for the search engines to know what each page of your site is about. This will let people scan through the search results they get allowing them to quickly determine if your web page contains what they are actually looking for. Also, you should remember that the page title is also what is used in order to link to your site from the results provided by the search engines.

It is important to ensure that the title on the page is one of your most important elements of your site. In fact, some people will argue that this is the most important part of any web page, above all other things.

Use of Real Headings

This is where you need to use h1-h6 (header tags) elements for your headings. By using graphics for your headings you are able to use any typeface you want (but search engines will not pay much attention to this). Even if you do use the alt attribute to specify an alternate text for heading images, this is not anywhere near as important as using real text in a heading element.

If you are unable to use real text for any reason, instead look at the various image or Flash replacement techniques that are available. Be aware though that there may be some risk involved in doing this. As image replacement involves hiding text, it is quite possible that you may be penalized by search engines for doing this, though, at this time, this kind of risk seems pretty slim.

Ensure that your URL is Search Engine Friendly

It is important to use a search engine friendly URL as opposed to a dynamically generated one that has a query string (which lets the server know which data to fetch from a database). Unfortunately, there are many search engine robots that have difficulties with this kind of URL and they may well stop at the question mark, and so not actually look at the entire query string.

By using a search engine friendly URL; you are helping both your ranking and users of your site. Many sites have seen an incredible improvement just because they have changed their URL scheme. Keep in mind, the modification and rewriting of a site's URL can be a little tricky.

Getting Linked

Really, the only good way to ensure that your site gets linked is to ensure that it contains good content. For any site on the web, incoming links are very important, especially for Search Engine Optimization. In fact, you may find that this is the hardest part of SEO for you to implement. Though considered important by most, many site owners have found that incoming links are less important, especially where you have more specific and unique content on your site.

Make it Accessible to All

This is as important as all elements previously mentioned. It is important that you make your website accessible to all, including those who are visually impaired. This comes with the welcomed side effect of helping search engine robots find their way around your website. It is important to remember that Google is blind. So, even if you are not concerned whether blind people can use your site or not (which we all should be in today's world) you still need for it to be accessible. What this means is that you should use real headings, paragraphs and lists and avoid using anything which may interfere with the search engines spiders.

Be Careful When Making a Submission

Although this is often overrated, submitting your site to directories and search engines can actually be useful. This is especially important if the site happens to be new and has not as yet been picked up by Google or the many other search engines that are around.

If you do want to look at submitting your website to directories, you may want to consider using the Yahoo! Directory and Open Directory Project as well as some directories specific to your topic (for example, if you have a blog, try submitting to http://www.blog-search.info). However, you will need patience as it can take several weeks for any submissions to be processed unless you pay to be listed.

Do Not Try to Fool the Search Engines

Never use such methods as cloaking, link farms, keyword stuffing, alt text spamming or any other dubious mannerisms. Although they may work for a short time, you not only risk getting your site penalized, but it actually could be banned from specific search engines altogether. Search engines like their results to be accurate and typically don't take kindly to people trying to trick them.

Avoid the Use of Frames

Although it is possible to provide workarounds that will allow a search engine robot to crawl frame based websites, these types of sites will still cause problems for any visitors who find it through a search engine. What happens is that when someone follows a link from a search result to a frame based site, they end up on an orphaned document. This will, in most cases, create confusion for the user, as in many cases vital parts of the site, such as navigational links, will be lost.

Browser Detection – Be Careful

If you have to use some kind of browser detection, then make sure that it doesn't break when a search engine spider or any other unknown agent comes along. Unfortunately, if the spiders can't get in, then your website will never be found.

Don't Waste Your Time with Meta Tags

You will find that most viable search engines today do not place a great deal of value on the content contained within Meta Tags. This is because they have been used and abused too much by spammers. So instead, if you need to, use Meta description elements. Although keywords will not hurt, they don't really help either, so generally it is not worth the effort to use them.

Often there are some search engine sites which will use the content of a Meta description element to describe a site in their search result listings. So whenever possible, make their contents unique and descriptive for every document or page.

As stated at the beginning of this chapter, we have provided a few basic guidelines in relation to SEO. But, there is much more that can be done in order to increase your website's visibility with search engines.

What is the Basic Link Structure within a Website?

This is probably the most obvious, yet still one of the most overlooked aspects of search engine optimization. This helps to make certain that search engine spiders can actually find (crawl) all of your website's pages. If they can't find your site's pages, then they won't get crawled, and this means that they won't get indexed. In fact, no amount of search engine optimization you try will help at this point.

Below are some points that should be looked at in regards to the link structure for your site.

Spiders can't see links which are accomplished by JavaScript. This is because, as far as search engines will be concerned, they simply don't exist. So if you want spiders to follow the links on your website, don't use JavaScript. In fact, you will find that Google will not crawl any URL if it looks like it has a session ID in it. So, any URL that has a longish number or odd characters (such as a question mark) in it should be avoided (this is often a dynamic URL).

It is important to you make sure that all webpages link to at least one other page on your website. Pages which do not link out are known as "dangling links." It's important that you structure the internal links so that targeted search terms are reinforced. So, be sure that you organize your links so that your topic's sub-topic pages are linked to it (ensuring that you use the right link text that is specific to the page being linked to) and vice versa. See below for the different types of methods we mean.

Link Text (<a href="url">some link text</a>

This is one of the two most important elements for ensuring good rankings for a site. It can either be on pages within your website, or on other websites' pages. But, whichever way you go about it, it is important that it is included. It is vital that you include the target page's main search term in the link text whenever possible and also avoid using identical text for every link that links to a page. In fact, links will carry more weight with search engines if the text around them is concerned with the target page's topic and search term(s).

Title Tag <title>some title words</title>

This is probably the second most important element in order to get good rankings for your web site. It is imperative that you make sure the page's search term is contained within this tag. So, place it as close to the front as possible while still ensuring that the title reads well. In fact, there is nothing wrong with you placing the search term up front on its own and then follow it with a period such as

"Page Rank. Google Page Rank and how do I make the most of it?" As you can see, the target search term here is of course "Page Rank". Make sure that each page's title tag is different from the title tags on your site's other pages.

Description Tag <meta name="description" content="a nice description">

You will find that some search engines, such as Google, no longer display the description as they use to. But no matter what, you should include this on each page for the search engines that still do. There are even the odd times when Google will actually display them. So it is vital that you write a description that is appealing and incorporates the page's search term into it at least once, or twice, which is even better. If you can, place one at the start or as near to the start of the description as possible.

Keywords Tag <meta="keywords" content="some keywords">

It is important to remember that the keywords tag is never actually treated by search engines as keywords. They will be treated as text on a page. Although this tag is not as effective as it used to be, there is no reason to leave it out. Instead, make sure that you put in plenty of relevant keywords and include the search term once at the front of the tag. Also, you shouldn't separate keywords or key phrases with commas (as is often done) as search engines ignore this.

H Tag <Hn>some heading words</Hn>

The "n" in this tag represents a number from 1 to 6, with the biggest heading is represented by 1. You will find that H tags are given more weight than ordinary text on a page, and so the bigger the H size, the more weight it will have. So it is important that you include your target search term in the H tags at least once on the page. If possible two or three times is even better. Also, place your first H Tag as near to the top of a website page as possible.

Bold Text

This gives more weight to a page than ordinary text, but not as much as an H Tag does. So, wherever possible, enclose the search term in bold tags where it appears on the page.

Normal Text

As often as you can, use the search term on the pages of your site. But, ensure that they don't detract from how the page actually reads. Ensure that you use the term once or twice in the very early pages of the text body, and then as often as possible throughout. If you need to, reword small parts and add sentences to ensure that the search term is well represented in the text for proper search engine optimization. You will probably find that each word you have in your search term will be found separately on the page. So, if you need to, add a few of them throughout the page.

Alt Text <img src="url" alt="some alt text which is displayed or mouseover">

Include your search term in the alt text of all images on your pages. It's important to remember that some systems, such as those used by Braille readers and speech synthesizers, use the alt text. So it may be advisable to make them usable while including the search term.

In summary, what you need to do is as follows:

1. Select the main search terms you wish to use.

2. Allocate these search terms to a suitable existing page, and if you need to, split pages.

3. Organize your internal links, and then your link text, to suit the target search terms and their pages.

4. If you can, organize those links from other pages to suit the target search terms and their pages.

5. Organize all the on page elements so they suit each page's target search term.

6. Sit back and watch your website's page rankings begin to improve.

Effective Use of Keywords for SEO

What you need to realize is that Search Engine Optimization does not need to be complicated. What you should do is make sure that each and every page of your website is a unique entity and is being treated in the appropriate manner where SEO is concerned. Below we provide you with some guidelines which should help you achieve your desired SEO results.

Get the Keywords Right

It's vital that the selected words you use meet your marketing criteria. So, don't pick words which are too general. Using words that are more specific will result in a higher ranking for your site. Also, it is important that you choose words which are suitable to your website. For example, you will find that "optimizing search engines" and "search engine optimization" have completely different rankings.

Include Keywords in your Page Titles

Unfortunately, a lot of people will use either use inappropriate names or their company name in the web page's titles. So, it's essential that you include the appropriate keywords in your title as that's the way people carry out searches on the internet.

Inclusion of Keywords in your Title Tags and Meta Tags

It is vital that, for each page of your site, you include the appropriate keywords within all the page's tags. Also, take the time to go over the Meta description that you use. You should make sure any description you use is alluring and interesting to those who are visiting your site, and include keywords within it wherever possible. There are many search engines around today which use the Meta description as a portion of what will be displayed in their search results.

Keywords in Content

It's significant for you to make sure you include keywords in the content of your website. But, don't overly do this, as too many will result in your page being discounted by the search engines.

When using these basic guidelines in relation to keywords and search engine optimization, you will find that your website can't help but be affected in a positive way.

How to Determine the Keyword Selection for Your Website

Making a website attractive to search engines is a key factor for its success. One of the key ways in which to rank well with search engines is by optimizing the visible keywords on the site's web pages. But, in order to be successful in your keyword strategy campaign, you should use the following two steps.

Keyword Selection

You will need to determine what your pages are offering and also determine which words your potential visitors might use in order to search for the pages of your website. You then need to create keywords which are based on those words.

For the full optimization of keywords on your website, you should use between three and five keywords on the appropriate pages. It is vital that you start using them from the top left and then down. Many times you will find that this will be the first 200 words on each page of your site, which will include the title tag, headings, abstract and so on. So, the closer to the top left of your page the keywords are placed then the more weight they will be given by Google. Often, visitors will view your site in the same way that the search engine spiders do, so emphasizing your keywords from the top left and down is a good way to design your website.

If your pages are already built, you may be thinking it is too late to select your keywords, but it's not. It doesn't matter if you choose your keywords before or after the site has gone live (although it is better to do it before as you will not need to rewrite the text on the pages). But if it is live, you may have the keywords, but they may not be the right ones. Yet they could be, and you have not fully utilized their optimization value. By using a thorough keyword selection process, you can make sure that they keywords you are using are optimized to their fullest extent.

A big issue where keyword selection is concerned is determining whether the keyword is too popular or competitive for you to use. If you find websites that are already ranking high and competing for particular keywords you might want to target, then you may need to select more specific keywords instead. This can also be said for keywords which have several different meanings. Therefore, it's important that you look how users will search for your pages, and which specific questions the content of your pages actually answers. Whenever possible, refine the keywords that you use in order to answer these questions.

When refining your keywords, it is important that you keep in mind that a large portion of searches carried out on the net contain three words or more. So, when people are searching for answers on the internet, they will often phrase their search term as a question. However, many people will not use search words that describe the solution to a question, but you can optimize your pages to their fullest extent if you think like the person who is searching.

Check Out the Competition

This is a great way of getting ideas. You do this by carrying out a search using keywords that you already know and that you would like to target. Click through the top sites that come up as a result of this search and once on a site, view their source HTML code and view the keywords that they have in their Meta tags. It's important that you remember to use the keywords which relate to your site or page. In order to view a site's HTML code, all you do is click on the "View" button at the top of your web browser page and then select "Source" or "Page Source".

By developing a list of keyword phrases, you should be able to optimize each page of your site for the search engines.

Please note: Some of the keyword above are misspelled on purposed. Sometimes commonly misspelled words also have high search volume and people looking for a business that provides your products and services.

What is Search Engine Friendly Content?

In this chapter, we will look at what search engine friendly content really is. Although you may think it is about stuffing your website with target keywords, it's far more involved. In fact, you may find that search engines call foul of the search if you solely focus on keyword stuffing. What you need to remember is that you need to write copy that will appeal to the search engine spiders, and be appealing to the human eye as well. After all, what is the point of having a website that is highly ranked if it is unappealing to all who visit it? So, it is vital that your site is user friendly to both your visitors, and not just the search engine spiders.

First of all, you need to answer the following questions:

1. What is your website for?

2. What does your website do?

3. What do you want your visitors to do when they reach your website?

4. Would you like visitors to spend money when they get to your website?

5. Are you just providing visitors with information?

These questions must be answered as they will have an impact on the copy that you write for the content of your website. So, whenever possible, use short paragraphs or bullet points, as these are more likely to attract visitors while more lengthy essays will only drive them away.

If you are selling a service or product, then you must also make your site look interesting. For example, provide as many calls to action as you can, and don't just provide visitors with an online price list.

It's important to remember that while you are trying to attract the search engines, but your site should be designed first and foremost for human readers. As long as a site has been designed well with people in mind, then 9 times out of 10 you will find that it is search engine friendly as well.

Just like a visitor to your site reads the copy on your page in order to figure out what you have to offer, so too does a search engine. So when a search engine is looking at your page, they are looking for keyword phrases in your copy (Content).

Below are a number of tips which will help you ensure your website's content is using proper SEO techniques.

1. You should have at least 200 words of copy on each page of your website. Although this may be difficult at times, search engines really like it, so it is important that you increase the amount of copy where you are able to. Generally speaking, once you surpass 1,000 words, the search engines will pretty much stop looking...so no need to get too long, unless the desired action you want from the visitor requires such action. This text, wherever possible, should include your most important keyword phrases, but should still remain logical and easy to read by visitors to the site.

2. Ensure that you use the phrases which you have used in the other tags on the pages during this part of the optimization process.

3. Add additional copy filled pages to the site, such as how to articles, tips or tutorials. Not only do these types of pages help with SEO, but you may find that other sites will link to yours.

These tips should not be ignored, as optimizing your web page copy (content) is one of the most important things you can do in order to improve your rankings in the search engines.

How do Backlinks Help with SEO?

A backlink is a link that directs others towards your website. They are also often referred to as inbound links (IBLs), and the number of backlinks your site has is an indication of how popular and/or important it is according to your peers (other website owners). These are especially important for SEO as search engines such as Google will give more credit to those sites with a good number of quality backlinks. So, they will consider such sites more relevant than others in the results pages of a search query.

Most search engines will want websites to have a level playing field, and will more often than not look for natural links that have been built slowly over time. Although it can be fairly easy to manipulate the links on a web page in order to achieve a higher ranking, it is a lot harder to influence a search engine with external backlinks from another site. This is why these feature factor in so highly in a search engine's algorithm.

Today it has gotten even harder to achieve these inbound links because of unscrupulous webmasters. Such people try to achieve these links by deceptive or sneaky techniques (through either hidden links or through automatically generated pages). These pages are known as link farms, and they are generally disregarded by search engines. In fact, if you are linked to such a link farm, then you may find your site being banned entirely from these search engines.

Another way of achieving quality backlinks to a site is to entice quality visitors to come to yours. There are a number of ways in which this type of back linking can be achieved.

1. **Reciprocal Linking.** This is where you link to another site that provides the same or a complimentary service or product as you and they in turn have a link to your site on theirs.

2. **Site Submissions.** Submit links for your website to directories which allow free submissions, or if you can afford it, some paid directories. There are many sites around which offer a service where you can submit your site details to numerous websites. Plus, if you want, you can always create your own directory of similar websites.

3. **Articles.** This is another way of getting great backlinks. If you have a reputable looking site that contains informative, well written articles and/or reviews, then there is a good

chance that your articles will receive high search engine rankings. It is vital that any articles you write are on subject, informative and thorough in relation to your site. Also, you could always write a few articles for submission to article sites such as EzineArticles.com or SearchWarp.com. This is another great way of gaining additional backlinks to your website.

Below are a few tips that should help you write quality articles for your site.

- Write in a way so that your intended target audience will understand what you are trying to say. In other words, don't write it as though you were a teacher talking to a class of 10 year olds, but don't be overly complicated either.

- Watch your spelling, grammar and punctuation. If in doubt, then use your spell checker and have someone else proof read your work.

- Don't make your articles too long. Usually, a good article will consist of between 350 to 500 words.

- Always include a resource box at the end, as this will include that all important backlink to your website. This resource box should also include a short biography regarding you and your website.

4. **Blogging.** This has now become an integral part of the internet and is one of the most effective ways of linking. You either have the choice of placing a few words or comments on to someone else's blog, or you may want to link to them from your own blog. In fact, you will find that most blogs will be happy to link back to you. However, it is important that you try to update your blog regularly and post interesting content to ensure that people will want to link back to you.

Conclusion

As you will soon see, search engines are one of the primary ways in which internet users will find a particular website. That's why a site with good search engine listings is likely to see a dramatic increase in the traffic that it receives.

Although everybody wants good listings, there are, unfortunately, many sites which appear poorly or not at all in search engine rankings. This is because they have failed to consider just exactly how a search engine works.

In particular, they forget that submitting to search engines is only part of the equation when you are trying to get a good search engine ranking for your website. Therefore, it is important that you prepare your website using proper search engine optimization techniques. This ensures that the pages of your site are accessible to search engines and are focused in such a way that they will help themselves improve their chances of being found by the search engine spiders.

PAID ADVERTISING STRATEGIES
GETTING PROFITABLE RESULTS

Using Pay Per Click (PPC) to Your Advantage

Targeting your customers with Pay Per Click can be a very stressful process for most business owners. Success demands a clear understanding of the seasonality, trends, and competition. You can get everything you need to know here.

PPC Basics

Harness the power of PPC through fully understanding it. Those who search online for the products and services you offer typically follow a common buying cycle: research, shop and purchase. Savvy marketers understand this cycle, the mindset of searchers in each segment of the sales funnel, and the importance of connecting with future buyers in their current phase and moving them closer to the purchase. A successful PPC campaign will not always move directly from search to purchase; immediate conversion is not always possible, and should not always be the goal. Using a spectrum of keywords reflective of the sales cycle for your products or services will yield better results than you would get by going for the immediate sale.

The Basics

Basically, PPC involves paying for website traffic. Advertisers pay each time a PPC ad they run is clicked on. A prospective buyer performs a search online using a keyword or keyword phrase relevant to the product or service they seek – most often searching from a consumer mindset, seeking a solution to a problem. A well-crafted PPC ad campaign will cause an advertisers PPC ad to appear in response to the prospect's query, and compel the searcher to click the ad and reach the advertiser's website. Ideally, the advertiser has built an effective landing page that assures the prospect they have reached a potential solution for their problem. The landing page should cause the searcher to start the process of knowing, liking, and trusting the site owner and believing the advertiser understands the nature of the problem and has an ideal solution for it.

Choosing a Search Engine

All of the major search engines cater to PPC advertisers. Each search engine's PPC program runs a bit differently. What works on one may not yield the same results on another search engine. Advertising fees, ad placement, and potential click counts vary among the search engines. Your results will vary, based on daily spending budget and receivable clicks, and not just bid amounts. Setting a budget for your PPC campaign is crucial; measuring each campaign's effectiveness on each search engine is also vital to getting the best results possible. This can be made easier by using a budget management tool, which can be reinitialized automatically once a PPC campaign runs its course.

Determine Your Target Market

This is very important as you do not want to throw money away on a bad PPC campaign. Ideally, you should first look at a target market that will favor your products and services, and then focus your PPC efforts on that group. When you aim for the correct target market, you will be able to effectively reduce your allocated budget, which will have the welcomed side effect of increasing your profit margin.

Know Your Market, Speak Their Language

Choosing keywords is the first consideration you should make when considering your target market. These keywords and phrases should work to lead your potential target market into your sales funnel, moving from merely interested to the point of being convinced there is no better solution to their problem or need. Though you could choose to use random keywords that are likely to get clicks, and thus traffic, that is not the kind of traffic you want. Random keywords that generate random clicks will not generate genuine interest, so your conversion rates will suffer as a result. It is far more effective to generate fewer clicks among more serious prospects than millions of clicks among people who have no genuine interest or intention to buy.

Of course, keywords alone do not make a PPC campaign a success. The triumph or failure of your PPC campaign comes from how you create your PPC advertisement. You'll want to create a PPC ad that is informative and attractive so you can generate the highest number of clicks possible among those who are truly interested in what you offer. For example, a seasonal PPC advertisement may be highly effective in driving traffic as the ad will be tailored to a specific target market.

Your target market will actually help you ensure more cost effective measures are taken, which is why the PPC platform is so popular for quick traffic. This is evident by looking at other businesses that pay far more for other types of advertising that are not as transparent and don't deliver results as good as PPC.

Choose Reputable PPC Providers

PPC is a very beneficial tool for advertising and online marketing as it enables a website to get ranked almost immediately through related search phrases. That in turn drives traffic in the form of targeted visitors. These visitors then become prospective buyers who can be urged to buy a product or service once they arrive at the advertiser's website.

Choose Well

There is always a possibility of losing money with an ill-conceived or poorly budgeted PPC advertising campaign. This makes finding reputable PPC providers to work with extremely important. Reputable PPC providers ideally have all the expertise that is needed to set up and manage all aspects of a specific PPC campaign to optimize the PPC style of marketing. Reputable PPC providers can help you get the most out of your PPC advertising dollar, ensuring high conversion rates and keeping your budget in check.

You'll know you're working with a quality PPC provider as they will see to it that you are consulted every step of the way. Additionally, they will ensure the proper keywords and key phrases are chosen for a specific PPC campaign, which should increase conversion rates, and the bottom line as a result.

It's important to conduct thorough research on any PPC provider you may be considering. You'll want to be certain they have a good reputation and inquire about their current client roster and track record. While the right PPC provider can help you out in almost every aspect of PPC marketing, the wrong choice can prove to do you more harm than good, particularly if you end up working with a PPC provider that practices click fraud, which is more prevalent than you might think.

Take your time choosing the right PPC provider. There is no need to rush the choice, and you shouldn't feel like you have to go with the first one you find. Conducting an interview will allow you to better understand each PPC provider you are considering and help you choose the right PPC provider for your PPC advertising campaign needs.

GOOD PROJECT MANAGEMENT IS ESSENTIAL

Running Your Practice vs. Managing Marketing Projects

It does not matter if you decide to do your own marketing or hire someone else. It is essential that you view each of your marketing campaigns as projects and track them using project management tools that keep things simple but ensures that you are successfully getting all the necessary task done in order to get optimum results.

In general, many of the tasks of an actively involved business owner are operational in nature. Operational activities are repeatable events and they are the tasks you perform routinely, such as taking care of new business, managing financial accounts, managing staff, and receiving phone calls from new customers or clients. A useful metaphor is to think of "operations" as the assembly line of your business.

Projects, on the other hand, are non-repeatable activities. Projects introduce new features to your assembly line. The Project Management Institute defines a project this way: "A project is temporary in that it has a defined beginning and end in time, and therefore defined scope and resources."

When you are considering setting up a local marketing campaign of any kind for your practice, some activities will be singular one-time projects, but you are also setting up a new, permanent operational channel that must be attended to on a regular basis. In summary, "local marketing projects" will involve creating new posts (updating your website, creating content, developing videos or digital media about new products or services). The most essential "local marketing activities" might be monitoring and managing your reputation by handling customer questions and complaints in order to avoid negative reviews on social media and local review sites.

The Two Most Important Local Marketing Projects

If you are starting at the beginning, there are two major projects required for setting up a social media marketing program for your small business. The first project should be Reputation Marketing, Monitoring and Management. It's essential that you are aware of what your clients are saying about our practice. There are 40+ local review sites (and hundreds of local niche sites) that allow your clients to post reviews about you and your business. Actively collecting positive reviews is critical. You have to make it easy for your clients to post good reviews about your business.

The second project is setting up and attracting followers to social accounts (i.e. Facebook, Google+, Twitter, etc.) and publishing marketing content to your followers and friends. When you collect good reviews, you should repost them on the various social sites. When you get negative or less than desirable reviews, you should proactively reach out to those new customers or clients to see if there is a way to resolve the issue and get them to change the rating for your business.

There are dozens of social media platforms for you to consider – Facebook, Foursquare, Twitter, YouTube, Google+, Vine, Instagram and on and on. Attempting to manage the projects and completing all of the task required to dominate a local area can be an overwhelming task if you are trying to do it all yourself. This is the perfect time to consider hiring someone to do it full time or hiring a "qualified" firm to get it done for you. Remember - your goal is to run your practice. Considering the number of tasks that need to be completed in order to expect positive and measurable results, it would be a major distraction if you sat in front of a computer to get this all done yourself.

Where to begin?

I suggest that you should start with these basic concepts to help guide your decision making process. Any given project management process takes into consideration:

- <u>Scope</u> (Where do you need to list your business and which social media platforms should you target?)

- <u>Time</u> (How much time to set up, and, more importantly, how much time to manage? Once set up, you must respond to customers in a timely fashion). This is where a good project manager or media consultant can be helpful.

- <u>Cost</u> (How much are you willing to spend to support your local marketing and social media campaigns? Will you handle all communications yourself, or will you hire someone to assist you? Will you invest in the right tools to help you manage your efforts?)

- <u>Quality</u> (Which local niche sites and social media platforms are best for your small business? Some may not be a good fit for your business and will not be worth the time to support.)

- <u>Communication</u> (How will you communicate your marketing efforts to employees and existing customers? You should have a communications plan to promote your new social media accounts to your customers.)

- <u>Risks</u> (What are the risks to using social media and other marketing platforms for your small business? Hint: the biggest risk is not having the discipline and support to respond in a timely fashion to customer questions, comments or complaints.)

- <u>Human resources</u> (Who will set up and operationally maintain your social media accounts?)

- <u>Creating Compelling Social Media Content.</u> This will set you apart from your competition. Your content should be focused on educating and keeping your clients informed of things within your industry that could have an impact on their health. For many, the most enjoyable aspect of owning social media sites is the opportunity to create content explaining your services or showcasing your products and employees. The possibilities are endless for marketing, promotion and having fun with your business.

It is difficult to make serious mistakes here, as long as one uses common sense. The basic rules are to focus on your business (not your personal life or opinions), remain patient focused (by taking into account good manners and maintaining a friendly demeanor), and always remember the purpose of social media is to create and maintain relationships. The key to success is making "compelling content." You customers want interesting or attractive content, and this requires planning.

The 5 Phases of Effective Projects

Knowing project management concepts can help. There are five major project management process groups that will help you structure your marketing efforts and content creation.

1. **Initiating** – For local and social media marketing, this includes the brainstorming phase. You should create a list of all possible campaigns planned for the month, including picture ideas, opportunities for positive testimonials from satisfied customers (written reviews and videos), photo ideas of your service in action or your product line (if possible). Offers and specials would be excellent promotions on your social media site. In this phase, you should also prioritize and schedule your best ideas, taking into consideration holidays or consumer shopping behavior based on time of the year.

2. **Planning** – Once you have a prioritized list of ideas, you can plan the details of each content element (i.e. picture or video). Good lighting, attractive locations and well-dressed employees, for example, must be planned in advance. You must also communicate with everyone involved what your expectations will be for a photo or video shoot. Ensure that your copy writing is error-free and grammatically correct. Make sure to put some time on your calendar to create this content, and stick to it for the sake of your social media program.

3. **Executing** – With proper planning in place this is straight forward. Once your content is complete, and you like it, post it!

4. **Controlling** – The controlling process for social media marketing is about measuring and tracking your successes and failures. You need to define both (failure and success) in order to make this process meaningful. On the one hand, a great success is a post that people like, +1, or share with others. But if you don't get the engagement you want, realize that customers will research your business online as part of their purchasing decision. An up-to-date social media presence that is open to public comment and criticism will raise the confidence of consumers to work with your business. (Note: Keep track of what your social contacts are engaging with so that you can adjust your strategy to increase future customer interactions.) On the other hand, failure is breaking your discipline of posting regularly and not responding to customer questions and complaints. The biggest failure is to break the rules of friendliness, good manners and maintaining business focus.

5. **Closing** – You should select a period of time to review your progress (perhaps monthly or quarterly) to review whether the social media marketing campaign is meeting your goals. Past experience shows that it takes some time for your social media program to achieve success. Your overall objective should be to see an increase in customer interaction and new customers walking through the door. Be sure to ask new customers if they are aware of your social media sites. In this closing phase, review what content was compelling to your customers, and thank employees or customers who helped create that content.

Essential Activities

The major operational activity that you need to consider is customer relationship management. During the day and early evening, you should acknowledge (not necessarily resolve) all customer questions and complaints within two hours. Customers consider interaction on social media to be similar to placing a phone call or sending an email. The fact that these interactions are public (and visible to everyone on the social network) makes their priority perhaps even more important than one-on-one phone calls or emails. Social media operations are about building relationships with your customers. All your project efforts aim at creating this channel of communication with your customers and the general public. Consumers expect this accountability and transparency, and if you can provide it, you will have an advantage over your competitors who do not. At the end of the day, maintaining an 5 star reputation is what will help you lead your competition in your local area.

To Check Out Your Reputation for FREE
Go To
http://www.MyReputationDenders.com

RESOURCES & MARKETING TOOLS

HTTP://LOCALMARKETINGFORSMALLBUSINESS.COM

ABOUT THE AUTHOR

Clarence Williams has spent most of his professional career in business consulting, information technology, sales and business development. Working with and coaching small business owners, his goal has always been to find ways to bring big company applications and solutions to the small and medium business community.

As the founder of Push Button Local Marketing, LLC., he's spent the last 7 years focused on local marketing strategies, techniques and tools that Small business owners can use to dominate a local area. The goal of the firm is to partner with one small business in your industry and local area to implement strategies that lead to profitable new customers or clients.

We expect our clients to dominate their local area within 3 to 6 months. We limit our services to one Professional in an area because working with more than one would make it difficult to get solid results and a clear return on investment for our clients. So before we bring on a new client, we will perform a complete marketing assessment and competitive analysis of their local area. This allows us to evaluate the potential returns we can expect and set our clients expectations accordingly.

Our marketing campaigns are designed to help you achieve the greatest return on investment. If we don't see a way to get you on the front page of the search results and keep you there, we will let you know that up front. This books was written so you don't have to spend your hard earned money on consultants and marketing efforts that will not lead to new business. Most of the strategies in this book are things you can do yourself. Nonetheless, our clients hire us so they can focus on their core business while we focus on helping them generate new business.

http://LocalMarketingForSmallBusiness.com

www.ingramcontent.com/pod-product-compliance
Lightning Source LLC
Chambersburg PA
CBHW071115210326
41519CB00020B/6299